CURRENCIES
that buy
CREDIBILITY

by Tom Wanek

PRESS

Austin, Texas

For my parents,
Tom and Michele Wanek,
who have always encouraged
me to swing for the fences.

Printed in Canada

Wizard Academy Press
16221 Crystal Hills Drive
Austin, TX 78737
512.295.5700 voice, 512.295.5701 fax
www.WizardAcademyPress.com

Ordering Information:
To order additional copies, contact your local
bookstore, visit www.WizardAcademyPress.com, or call
1.800.425.4769
Quantity discounts are available.

ISBN: 978-1-932226-76-8

Library of Congress Number: 2009937162

Book cover design by Myra Falisz

First printing: October 2009

Acknowledgments   7

Part One - The Basis For Credibility

Chapter 1 - More than Words   13

Chapter 2 - Signaling Theory:
The Foundation for Credibility   19

Chapter 3 - Crafting Believable Messages:
The Six Currencies that Buy Credibility   29

Part Two - Currencies In Action

Chapter 4 - Currency: Material Wealth   37

Chapter 5 - Currency: Time & Energy   51

Chapter 6 - Currency: Opportunity   65

Chapter 7 - Currency: Power & Control   77

Chapter 8 - Currency: Reputation & Prestige   89

Chapter 9 - Currency: Safety & Well-Being   107

Part Three - Tying It All Together

Chapter 10 - The Three Questions of
Message Alignment   119

Chapter 11 - The Anatomy of a
Power Statement   129

Chapter 12 - Final Thoughts   147

About the Author   152

Bibliography   153

What is Wizard Academy?   158

Acknowledgments

Writing a book is a solitary experience. Early mornings and late nights buoyed by a boatload of caffeine.

But this author couldn't pen a meaningful thought without the support of his family, friends and colleagues. And this kind of support is worth a fortune. I therefore hope that the following acknowledgments will serve in lieu of cash:

To my best friend and wife, Lydia. Even though I encouraged you to run straight for the hills, you never once objected to my boundless ambition. And you, more than anyone, had to endure my endless babbling about the contents of this book. I appreciate your love, patience and support.

A special thanks to my two beautiful daughters, Olivia and Eva. I'll never forget those countless times you moseyed on down to my office to ask me how the book was progressing. I love you both.

I am incredibly grateful to Roy and Pennie Williams. This book would not exist without either of you. You encouraged me to throw my cap over the wall, kill the ox and burn the plow, and run toward the sound of the guns. Thank you for waking that quiet ferocity within me.

I thank my parents, Tom and Michele Wanek. You have given me a lifetime of encouragement and support – even when it came at your expense. Well, it's payback time.

And thank you to Myra Falisz. I couldn't have hired a better editor for this book. Not only did you sharpen my words, but you helped to bring out my best ideas. This book is far better because of your input.

Thanks to Corrine and Sean Taylor, and the rest of the staff at Wizard of Ads, Wizard Academy and Wizard Academy Press. A heartfelt of thanks for the encouragement I received from my friends and partners: Dave and Julie Young, Craig and Angela Arthur, and Michele Miller. And to all of my Wizard of Ads partners, thank you for your helpful comments and advice.

Part One:
The Basis For Credibility

One thing we can all agree on — there's a lot of bullshit in the ad business. As a matter of fact, if it wasn't for presidential candidates, art critics, and branding consultants, we would lead the league in bullshit.

- Bob Hoffman, *The Ad Contrarian*

Chapter One
More than Words

"Oh, don't worry she won't bite."

Yeah right. Do you really expect me to believe that?

It's a line I hear – without fail – at least once a week from enthusiastic dog owners as I jog through my neighborhood. And although it's been 11 years since an angry German Shepherd sunk his teeth into my leg – an experience that's forever bleached into my memory – I remain skeptical whenever I hear dog owners offer such reassurances.

I need more than words. And your customer's view of marketing is a lot like this.

Whether it's caused by one big chomp or smaller nibbles over time, your customer turns a doubtful eye towards marketing and advertising. Past instances of ploys and gimmicks alert her brain. And your customer uses these memories to guide her buying decisions.

But that's not all: Your customer also relies on the collective memories of all consumers – through what's commonly known as word of mouth. And the Internet is a word-of-mouth megaphone that gives truth-thirsty customers a lightning-fast way to model the experiences of others. So companies today have nowhere to hide. And that's why the old assumptions of marketing – that you can overpower your customer with ad-speak and hype – are doomed.

But hey, don't take my word for it. Here's proof: *The 2008 Edelman Trust Barometer* reports that only 22 percent of young Americans (ages 25 - 34) say product and corporate advertising is a credible source of information. Topping it off, product and corporate advertising ranked lowest on the credibility scale of any information source surveyed.

Surprised? *I didn't think so.*

But please don't misinterpret this data as
meaning advertising is ineffective; that
you're destined to see lame results. And
allow me to be clear: I'm not suggesting
you refrain from advertising. *Nonsense.*
What the Edelman data says – in a
nutshell – is that most ads today lack
believability. And it's the absence of
believability that should give marketers a
smack-you-between-the-eyes wake up call.

The Edelman report adds, "Companies
would be wise to pay more attention to
fostering trust in advance and gaining
an understanding of its depth among its
audiences. Both will provide some security
during a time of uncertainty and change
– especially when the economy takes a
downturn. By protecting a company's
license to operate, trust can serve as a
catalyst for a company's growth. Without
it, a company loses that license."

Fostering trust. Now there's a garden-of-

Eden breath of fresh air that is all too often ignored or forgotten in business and marketing. The importance of trust cannot be underestimated – especially in light of scandals such as Enron, the sub-prime housing bailout, or the disgraced money manager Bernard Madoff.

Neurologists are now discovering that humans are uniquely gifted to detect and respond to trust in other humans. We use these abilities to reduce uncertainty or avoid risk and the pain of loss. Which means your customer relies on these same abilities when making buying decisions.

What can you do about it? How can you craft believable marketing messages and gain the trust of your customers?

I'm glad you asked.

But first allow me to warn you up front: If you want to learn about the latest step-by-step marketing craze, *this book isn't for you.*

Earning your customer's trust requires

taking your marketing beyond quick fixes and hit-and-run techniques. It requires an iron backbone and relentless determination. And most importantly – as I'll soon explain – it requires an investment that goes beyond words.

Have you got the goods?

Moving forward, you'll learn insights and principles – based on science – that will elevate your company's credibility and earn your customer's trust. And as we saw from the *Edelman Trust Barometer*, fostering trust goes a long way in persuading customers to buy from you.

But before I share those principles, it will be helpful for you to appreciate exactly *why* these principles work and *where* they originate. And that's how we'll begin.

So roll up your sleeves. Let's get to work.

To gauge the reliability of the signal, then,
one has to consider the investment it entails.
The cost – the handicap the signaler takes on –
guarantees that the signal is reliable.

- Amotz Zahavi, *The Handicap Principle*

Chapter Two

Signaling Theory: The Foundation for Credibility

Animals have no words. But would it surprise you to learn that animals communicate using methods that are more believable and trustworthy?

For more than three decades, biologists have known that trust understands a language that does not rely on words. Their Signaling Theory research painstakingly observes how animals rely on bizarre behaviors and physical traits to communicate with honesty and trust. And here's why you should care: The principles of Signaling Theory can be successfully applied to anyone's marketing strategy. Straightforward communication boosts your credibility and earns your customer's trust. *At full-tilt.*

Have I got your attention?

Great. Let's take a crash course in Signaling Theory to uncover what it takes to become credible. Now you might be concerned that our venture into biology will leave you dazed and confused. Don't worry, I promise to make Signaling Theory easy-to-understand. So let's keep on trucking.

The Gazelle and the Cheetah:

The life and death exchange between the gazelle and the cheetah provides us with a striking example of Signaling Theory.

Swift and darting, the gazelle can quickly change directions and run over long distances at a top speed of 50mph. But before we declare the gazelle a wonder of nature, you should know that its main predator – the cheetah – sprints at an eye-blazing 70mph.

Poor little gazelle.

Faced with an overwhelming disadvantage in speed, it becomes obvious why most gazelles twitch and run at the slightest hint of danger. But hold on a second. Not all gazelles bolt for safety upon noticing a stalking cheetah. *Occasionally*, a small number of emboldened gazelles actually begin stotting when standing face-to-face with the deadly cheetah. Stotting is the act of leaping up and down repeatedly while stiffening all four legs. That's right. Lock. Leap. Repeat.

So why would a gazelle stot? What would prompt such unthinkable, energy-zapping, risky behavior ... instead of spending its resources to escape the cheetah's lightning-fast attack?

It's a question that's baffled evolutionary biologists for nearly 150 years – since the publication of Charles Darwin's *On the Origin of Species*. Here's the reason: Darwin's Theory of Natural Selection

suggests stotting is the
exact type of behavior
that should have become
extinct long ago. Yet,
stotting is alive and well
today.

With no solid
explanation – other than
stotting gazelles are deranged – biologists
remained mystified. Until 1975, when
Israeli biologist, Amotz Zahavi, presented
The Handicap Principle as an explanation
for stotting, and other bizarre animal
behaviors and physical traits. Zahavi's
theory suggests that stotting – a display
of athleticism and endurance – sends a
distinct, direct message that the gazelle
can outrun and outlast the cheetah.
Because the gazelle squanders precious
time and energy, the signal reverberates
with a *high degree of believability*.

But what about the cheetah?

Knowing several weeks could pass before it
finds another opportunity to wrangle some

grub, the cheetah will *ignore* the stotting gazelle, instead turning its attention to those gazelles that immediately ran for safety. Here's why: The cheetah is hunting for the biggest meal it can find, while spending as little of its limited energy as possible. And, above all else, the cheetah seeks to avoid a pointless and exhausting chase.

But here's one important question that demands an answer: If stotting is so convincing – equating to a "Get Out of Jail Free" card – then why don't all gazelles stot?

Because stotting demands an investment not all gazelles can afford. For the vast majority of gazelles, the cost of stotting *outweighs* the benefit. And survival doesn't require one to be the herd's *fastest*. It simply requires being faster than the herd's *slowest*. Most gazelles don't stot because they're instinctively aware that any display of inferior athleticism would be painfully obvious next to superior stotters. That's not a healthy position to be in when you've just depleted all the resources needed to outrun the cheetah.

Here's another way to look at it: For gazelles of inferior athletic ability, the cost of signaling is too high. Why waste time and energy stotting – attempting to fool the cheetah while appearing weak among the herd? If you can't support what you're signaling, then don't send that particular signal. Redirect your resources.

And Signaling Theory isn't limited to the gazelle and cheetah. It exists in every corner of biology. Let's take a look at three more *brief* examples of Signaling Theory to boost your understanding.

The Peacock's Big, Bright Tail:

The peacock's tall, bright and colorful tail is a demonstration of strength and endurance. And the extra burden of the tail is metabolically costly. Only the strongest and healthiest peacocks can grow tall, bright and colorful tails.

The peacock's tail, then, is a signal of being a worthy mate to the peahen. The correlation is this: If a peacock is strong and healthy enough to lug around a cumbersome tail, it will have no problem caring for the peahen and their offspring.

That Dog Ain't Smiling!

It's said that one should never smile at a stray dog.

Why?

Because dogs don't smile. People do. Dogs bite.

And, showing your teeth is a motion that resembles biting. It's likely that the dog will interpret your smiling as a signal of confidence *and an invitation to fight*. The credibility of this signal – displaying your teeth – comes from the interpretation that you're willing to your risk safety and well-being.

Clumsy Antlers?

The spiraling racks of antlers that adorn male deer do not act as clumsy weapons. Like the peacock's tail, antlers are metabolically costly, requiring great strength and stamina to carry. Because only the strongest and healthiest males grow the large racks, antlers are a credible signal of a deer's worthiness as a mate to the female.

And it's important to note that antlers also serve as a signal of strength and fitness to rival males. These antlers are often displayed during fighting rituals. Fighting rituals involve movements and postures that *mimic* fighting. But contrary to popular belief, these rituals rarely escalate into real fights. Their primary purpose is to determine the stronger of two male rivals *without causing injury or harm*. The males instinctively know their individual chances of survival are greater if both remain healthy and unharmed.

Moving on:

If you understand one thing from Signaling Theory, please understand this: Investment – what you're willing to risk or spend – is the key to gaining credibility. When analyzing buying decisions, customers will weigh your investment in their minds.

So, now we're going leave our discussion of biology. It's time to show how Signaling Theory can be used to create powerful strategies and craft believable marketing messages.

The sight of action is an incentive for action.
        - From the book, *A Pattern Language*

Chapter Three

Crafting Believable Messages:
The Six Currencies that Buy Credibility

The ability to speak a structured language allows us to communicate complex ideas with relative ease. Yet your greatest strength is also your greatest weakness. That's why I'm convinced that speaking comes far too easily for words to communicate with a high degree of believability.

But after years of research and observation, I've determined that credibility can be *purchased* by investing in one or more of six currencies. And the more you risk or spend, the more *believable* your message becomes.

The Six Currencies
That Buy Credibility:

1. Material Wealth

Of the six currencies, we see material
wealth risked most frequently in
guarantees and warranties. Nordstrom's
guarantee is legendary. Companies like
Nordstrom reduce buyer uncertainty
and win loyalty with such statements as,
"Return the product at any time for a full
refund." How might your business take on
the buyer's risk to strengthen credibility?

2. Time & Energy

Home Depot spends time and energy
offering free in-store clinics on home
improvement topics such as "Tiling Floors
& Walls" and "Energy Efficiency In Your
Home." Can you think of a better way to
communicate your company's expertise?

3. Opportunity

Imagine a key employee turning down a higher-paying job offer from a competitor. Do you believe her now when she raves about working for your company?

Likewise, some manufacturers bypass the opportunity to sell their products in the big-box chain stores as a way to project an image of quality and prestige. Is there an opportunity you can intentionally bypass to boost your company's credibility?

4. Power & Control

Shopping for car insurance is dreadfully time consuming – like watching paint dry on a wall. To make the process easier and faster, Progressive Insurance offers comparison rate quotes online, including most rival insurance companies. By giving up power and control, Progressive communicates they are trustworthy and easygoing. How might your company invest power and control?

5. Reputation & Prestige

In November of 2008, The Big Three auto companies requested big bucks – $25 billion taxpayer bucks – to bail them out from a swirling mix of financial rot. But the CEOs of these companies each flew to Washington to ask for financial help *in their private jets.* Spending $20,000 per round-trip plane ride sent a thunderous message to lawmakers and taxpayers that these three companies either don't need our money – or more likely – are not responsible enough to spend it.

The public outrage was directly proportionate to this nearly deafening message. It's as if we can't even hear – let alone believe – your request because your actions are so far afield. Such a piercing sound can shatter one's reputation instantly.

By not flying commercial, the CEOs of the Big Three lost major credibility. Does your company wisely invest every action?

6. Safety & Well-Being

Some street gangs use an initiation rite called a "beat in" to determine if an inductee is mentally and physically strong enough to become a member. Inductees must risk safety and well-being by enduring a physical bashing from several gang members.

Richard Davis, the founder of bulletproof vest manufacturer Second Chance®, proves the safety of his product by shooting himself at point-blank range while wearing his company's body armor. He began risking his personal safety and well-being to demonstrate the stellar performance of his company's vests. It was 1971 – a time when no one believed a Kevlar vest could stop a speeding bullet. Since 1972, the company has tracked 1,000 documented "saves" among law enforcement professionals wearing its bullet-resistant vests. Do you walk the walk when it comes to your product or service?

Are you beginning to see how investing in these six currencies buys credibility? Next, we'll look at specific examples and explore how companies invest these currencies to earn credibility. We'll even come across a few train-wrecks along the way from companies who *fail* to invest when customers expect it.

Part Two:

Currencies In Action

Don't tell me where your priorities are. Show me where you spend your money and I'll tell you what they are.

- James W. Frick

Chapter Four
Currency: Material Wealth

One Hour Heating & Air Conditioning™:
On time service – guaranteed

Your home is a block of ice. Every exhale,
a vapor of frost. Your attempt to crank up
the heat is met with ominous sounds: *Hiss.*
Gurgle. Clank. Clunk.

Yes, your furnace is dying. No longer able
to stave off the insatiable maw of "Old
Man Winter."

Knowing better than to take matters into
your own hands, you do what thousands
of other mechanically challenged
homeowners do each year: (*GONG!!!*) You
call your local heating repair company.

Enter frustration.

Sure, they'll come out to your home and fix your furnace, *but only by further disrupting your life.* "Anytime between 8 a.m. and 5 p.m." is the closest you'll get to nailing down an arrival time. *Ugh!*

And forget about them showing up lickety-split, first thing in the morning. *Puh-leez. Just ain't gonna happen.*

So what will you do now? Lie to your boss and call in sick? Squander a vacation day? Take off work without pay? Oh well, that's your problem, *not theirs.* After all, someone has to be home to let the repair tech in, right?

Talk about a universally hated event. Being handcuffed to the technician's schedule is something we've all experienced. Amazingly, most in-home service companies completely disregard the customer's time, preferring to brag about being the "largest" or having the "highest-quality."

But not One Hour Heating and Air Conditioning. They became the nation's first heating and cooling service company to promise on-time service.

But how does One Hour inject *believability* into their promise?

By taking it beyond words.

One Hour's promise is anchored by their *"Always on time or you don't pay a dime"*® guarantee – *risking material wealth to buy credibility.* Here's how it works: Schedule an appointment and an experienced repair technician will show up at your home within a one-hour service window. If the technician arrives after the one-hour window expires – even just one teeny tiny second – the entire service call is free. *Including parts and labor.* To further ensure your time isn't wasted, each service truck arrives *fully stocked and loaded* with more than $15,000 in parts, avoiding those time-consuming trips "back to the shop."

Look at it this way: To diminish any doubt that their on-time promise is a ploy or gimmick, One Hour risks material wealth with a "no bull" guarantee. And like the life-on-the-line behavior of the stotting gazelle, the degree of investment – what you are willing to risk or spend – sends a *distinct, direct* message. The more you risk or spend, the more believable your message becomes. *Period.*

It's helpful to appreciate that warranties and guarantees are *the most common* currencies risked in business today. These reassuring measures illustrate the power of risk reversal, which occurs when the business reduces buyer uncertainty by assuming the financial risk of making a purchase.

But beware: not all warranties and guarantees are equally powerful. The most effective carve out a strategy, scaling your business to heights the competition is afraid to climb. And powerful guarantees are simple and specific. No fine print. No squirmy loopholes. No flaccid language.

By addressing a felt need – backed by a powerful guarantee – One Hour created a marketing strategy that's boomed their business. And it's no coincidence that the company enjoys a 90 percent closure rate on every in-bound call they receive. *Now that's impressive!*

And that's not all: One Hour Heating & Air Conditioning became Entrepreneur Magazine's #1 ranked heating and air conditioning franchise for 2008.

But hold on a second. Do you think this same strategy applies to other in-home service companies?

You bet it does.

Clockworks Home Services, Inc. – the parent company of One Hour Heating & Air Conditioning – has been using variations of this classic strategy to build a number of America's most successful in-home service franchises such as Mister Sparky Electrician and Benjamin Franklin Plumbing.

My friend and partner, Roy H. Williams, calls this Business Problem Topology. It's the process of identifying a parallel but unrelated business that faced a similar challenge, and adapting their solution to overcome yours. For example, Clockworks very well might have adapted the Fed-Ex or Dominos Pizza on-time delivery guarantee to its own delivery of on-time service.

Yes, creating bold, powerful statements is easy. But making these statements *believable* requires more than words. Like One Hour Heating & Air Conditioning, your company's credibility is directly related to your willingness to invest.

How can you risk or spend material wealth to reinforce the promises you make?

Jim Gilbert's Wheels and Deals:
A huggable car dealer?

When was the last time you felt any joy or affection when buying a used car?

I bet it's never happened. That's understandable. Just the thought is repulsive for most. Why would anyone want to hug a used-car dealer?

But it might surprise you to know that overjoyed customers are hugging Jim Gilbert *daily* at his Wheels and Deals used-car dealership in Fredericton, New Brunswick, Canada.

Jim's effect on customers is shocking because no other business on the planet is as universally detested as a used-car dealer. Most folks have no problem conjuring up a cascade of dreadful mental images when thinking of buying a used car.

You know the ones: A creepy sales guy

lurking next to the giant inflatable pink gorilla. The cheesy sales pitches, arm-twisting and gimmicks. Oh, and don't forget about the clunker that's destined to ignite into hellish flames soon after driving off the lot. *Okay, that last one was a bit dramatic.* But you get the picture.

So how does Jim Gilbert win the loyalty and affection of his customers? How does he convince the public that his dealership is credible – unlike any other used-car goobers we love to hate?

Jim Gilbert accomplishes this amazing feat by investing material wealth to send a believable message: His dealership sells dependable used cars.

In fact, Jim invests material wealth in two very different and compelling ways.

First, Jim's dealership attaches a six-month/12,000 kilometer warranty to *every vehicle sold.* Recall from the previous example that the most effective warranties carve out a strategy, taking your business to heights your competition is afraid to climb.

Jim's warranty does exactly that. No other used-car dealership in Fredericton has the guts to match Jim's warranty. And you can bet the competition is sitting back, smugly thinking that Jim Gilbert must be insane. They're just waiting for his dealership to go broke.

But Jim isn't insane. And his dealership isn't going broke.

Here's why: Jim doesn't risk or spend currencies with reckless abandon. He *budgets* for the investment by skipping out on the weekly, clichéd sales events. Jim's dealership doesn't have to play the discount game. The desire to buy a dependable used car is a felt need that attracts plenty of customers to Jim's dealership.

The second way Jim invests material wealth is perhaps more compelling than the first. Jim's built a state-of-the-art, Napa-Pro Service Shop on site. The service shop is outfitted with five bays, Napa-certified mechanics, computer diagnostic equipment and the latest tools. And you'll appreciate that Napa requires all authorized service shops to maintain a high level of competency. Jim pays for his mechanics to attend ongoing training sessions, keeping them up-to-date on the latest techniques, parts and equipment.

Here's what this means to Jim's customers: Every late-model used car Jim acquires goes through a complete and thorough inspection in its Napa-sanctioned service shop. Any and all repairs are made *before* the car is placed on the lot to be sold. This investment of material wealth transfers

confidence to the customer and speaks
directly to the reliability of the vehicles
Jim sells.

Making this strategy even more exclusive,
the dealership only services the vehicles
they sell. Knowing long wait times would
frustrate their car-buying customers, Jim
intentionally bypasses the opportunity to
make additional money by not opening his
shop to the general public.

Yes, Jim's playing with the big boys.

But allow me to be up front: I'm a colleague
of Ray Seggren, the Wizard of Ads consultant
who developed the brilliant marketing
strategy for Jim Gilbert's Wheels and
Deals. Although the idea of a "Huggable"
car dealer selling "New to You" vehicles
is quirky and gets one's attention, Ray
knows credibility must be purchased by
investing material wealth in Jim's warranty
and service shop. And he successfully uses

these two assets to drive the message home that Jim sells dependable used cars. That's why consumers vote Jim Gilbert's Wheels and Deals the #1 used-car dealership in Fredericton year after year. And that's why customers hug Jim.

Lost time is never found again.

– Benjamin Franklin

Chapter Five
Currency: Time & Energy

REI: Proving they are the world's outdoor equipment experts.

Some men are hunters, others fishermen. I'm a city guy.

But in 2003, I broke rank from my urban roots and decided to hike the Grand Canyon with a few of my closest buddies. Three days and two nights of sweltering heat, physical exertion, uncaged wildlife and dizzying heights.

Had I frazzled my neurons? My previous outdoor experience – backyard camping – was mere child's play compared to what surely awaited me.

Yes, I was backcountry rookie, but I quickly grasped that one has to prepare for the great outdoors. Otherwise, Mother Nature will slap you silly. You can find yourself off the beaten path, suffer a heat stroke or be swept away in a flash flood. These things happen quickly. And you can't just close your eyes, click your heels, and magically appear safely back home.

Here's the bottom line: Owning the right equipment can mean the difference between a pleasurable backpacking experience and complete misery. My plastic pop-up tent, old college backpack and Nike sneakers weren't going to make the cut. And visiting the local big-box chain store was an effort in futility. The goober managing the sporting goods department tried to sell me a George Foreman portable grill. *Go figure.*

Yes, finding the right gear was going to require a fair amount of research and effort.

So where does a city slicker go to get the inside scoop on buying the right outdoor clothing, doodads and gizmos?

The Internet. *Where else?*

Online, I stumbled upon the holy grail of outdoor articles and buying guides: REI.com (Recreational Equipment, Incorporated). The retailer invests *time and energy* to put together an exhaustively comprehensive expert-advice section for outdoor equipment and best practices.

On REI.com, you'll find seven major categories of outdoor advice, spanning Camping & Hiking, Climbing, Cycling, Outdoor Fitness, Paddling, Snowsports and Travel.

And let there be no doubt: REI doesn't slap together a bunch of powder-puff articles and guides. Nope, the retailer goes all-out. Its Camping & Hiking category, alone, is jam-packed with more than 90 topics rewarding the stymied outdoorsman with insider takeaways and *Ah-has!* at each and every turn. Learn how to choose hiking boots, what to do if you become lost or how to maintain proper hygiene on the trail – an absolute must if a shower is a comfort you can't live without.

Want even more hands-on training?

For an affordable price, REI's outdoor school offers detailed training from experienced instructors on the adventure that interests you.

But here's what's critical to understand: By investing an enormous amount of time and energy to educate visitors on the

outdoors, REI team members build trust and confidence in the recommendations they make and the products they sell. Because REI and its staff prove they're the world's outdoor-equipment experts, customers are more likely to buy from them.

Yes, some folks will use REI for its expertise only, then turn around and purchase their gear from a competitor. It happens. I'm sure. But REI is the leader in outdoor equipment because the company risks time and energy to arm visitors with expert knowledge. And I have yet to come across a retailer in any market or category offering as much free, valuable information as REI. Its initiative is unrivaled.

And you might appreciate that REI doesn't boast about being the "World's Best Outdoor Resource." You'll find no such claim on their web site. REI simply lets the heaping mountain of content do all the talking.

What better way to communicate one's expertise?

Sprint: No cellular service for you!

There's a classic episode of the hit sitcom, *Seinfeld*, where a local soup stand becomes all the rage. And like moths to a flame, Jerry, George and Elaine wait in line daily for a cup of their favorite liquid broth.

But there's just one catch: The trio must arrest their bumbling behavior and not upset the wacky owner. Nicknamed the "Soup Nazi," he insists that customers place their orders in a strict, regimented manner and is quick to ban his soup-loving patrons for committing the slightest infraction.

The Soup Nazi's ironclad rules: Select the soup you want. Be ready to pay. And move to your extreme left after ordering.

As you might recall, George finds himself in trouble when a piece of bread mistakenly goes missing from his order.

After politely informing the Soup Nazi of the omission, George is sternly told that the bread will now cost him an *additional* three dollars. Protesting, George demands to know why he has to pay when everyone else receives bread for free. In response, the Soup Nazi barks, "No soup for you!" George's order is snatched back and his money is promptly returned.

A story this fantastically ridiculous can only happen on television.

Yeah right.

On June 29th, 2007, Sprint fired 1,000 customers for calling the company's customer support line *too often*.

Yes, you read correctly.

Considering Sprint's customers had no idea that frequent calls were a breach of etiquette, the cellular company's actions were even more absurd than the Soup Nazi's. And Sprint's decision to whack pesky customers sent a booming message to wireless consumers nationwide: Sprint's customer support is a toxic pit of incompetence.

Why?

Because Sprint failed to invest *time and energy* to solve customer concerns. And as a result, Sprint's credibility plummeted.

Here's how it all went down: Sprint mailed a formal letter to terminated customers explaining, "The number of inquiries you have made to us during this time has led us to determine that we are unable to meet your current wireless needs." The company also notified these customers that they would be given exactly one month to find another wireless provider.

Now in fairness to Sprint, these 1,000

customers were demanding. In a year's time, each averaged 25 calls per month to Sprint's customer support line. *Yes, that's annoying by anyone's definition.*

And in the spirit of harmony, Sprint waived the "Early Termination Fee" and brought each customer's account balance down to zero.

Fair enough. But here's where things get wiggy: Sprint mostly dropped the ax on customers with accounts in good standing. And many of these customers had legitimate gripes about billing issues and technical glitches, which were directly related to Sprint's clumsy 2004 merger with Nextel.

The heart of the problem: Sprint and Nextel operated on two completely different technology platforms. And merging the two platforms became a nightmare for Sprint. After three years,

Sprint still had not eliminated all the kinks. *Not even close.*

Now let me be clear: I'm *not* suggesting there's never cause to fire a customer. Nonsense. Sometimes it's justified. I get it.

I'm simply recommending that you fully weigh the public's perceptions *and expectations* before sending *any* message.

Sprint failed to appreciate how the public might interpret its decision. Customers expect reputable companies to invest the time and energy to fix problems with their product or service. Sweeping problems aside by ousting a small contingent of high-maintenance customers only created disconnect and doubt.

Making Sprint's blunder even more pathetic: the widely known fact that crummy customer service plagues the wireless industry. According to *Cellular-News,* subscribers cite poor customer service as the primary reason for switching cell phone providers.

Not surprisingly, Sprint's ability to maintain and attract customers was crippled. Before the move, Sprint – the nation's third largest wireless provider – enjoyed more than 53 million subscribers. Within three months, its subscriber base had nose-dived to 41 million, which led to the firing of CEO Gary Forsee in October 2007. A year later, Sprint's subscriber base continued its free fall, with no leveling off in sight.

And Sprint's decision sent a second unintended message: Call the support line every day for a year straight, and you just might be able to wiggle out of your service contract without having to fork over big bucks for the early termination fee. Yep, Sprint just attracted the exact type of behavior it hoped to eliminate. *Oh the irony.*

In choosing one path we ignore others. And wonder what might have been.

— Binnesman

Chapter Six
Currency: Opportunity

Geppetto's Workshop:
No plastic. No Batteries.

Bright eyes point skyward. Little feet
scurry down the aisles. Grownups journey
back to their childhood. Geppetto's
Workshop is a toy store unlike any I've
ever seen.

Marionettes and puppets dangle from
the ceiling. Hand-crafted kaleidoscopes,
spinning tops and games pack the shelves.

Fun embraces you in every corner.

This charming little shop thrives under the crushing weight of toy giants, Wal-Mart and Toys "R" Us.

So how does Geppetto's fight the big boys and win?

By choosing which customers to lose.

Geppetto's refuses to stock toys made from plastic. And you won't find any of its gadgets requiring batteries. *Not a single one.*

It's a bold decision, making it unlikely that any of Geppetto's toys will be scribbled down on your kid's wish list. But hey, if all you want to do is distract little Johnny or Suzy with addictive lights and sounds, then Geppetto's prefers you shop someplace else.

Sound insane, gutsy or harsh?

Yes, choosing who to lose takes unwavering courage and commitment.

Geppetto's brushes aside any opportunity to pad its pockets by selling the season's "must-have" toys. And it skips out on the buying frenzy sparked by many of these items. It's a decision that costs Geppetto's a jackpot of sales. But it's a price the company willingly pays to stand out from the crowd.

Geppetto's understands that stockpiling the trendy toys would only taint their store. And no one would believe the company's commitment to nurturing a child's creativity if they did. *Not a soul.*

Geppetto's resists the temptation to

go commercial in an all-out effort to avoid becoming ordinary. Let's face it: Ordinary is the kiss of death for the small, independent retailer.

Here's the deal: Most folks will avoid shopping at Geppetto's simply because they don't stock the popular, commercialized toys. Yet the absence of these toys is exactly what attracts an army of shoppers right to Geppetto's door.

It's what my friend and partner, Roy H. Williams calls the Law of Polarity which states, "Your business' ability to attract customers cannot exceed its potential to repel."

Here's an example of an ad demonstrating Geppetto's credibility investment:

Plastic and batteries stifle a child's creativity. Toys with addictive lights and sounds manufacture an imaginary world for your child. Motors and electronics are a creative crutch.

Karaoke machines with flashing laser lights.
High-definition video games with movie-like graphics.
Intergalactic robots transforming into tiny little Toyota Corollas.

Want your child playing with these toys?

Then hit your local Wal-Mart.

Every year over-commercialized toys leap off the shelves onto the best-sellers list. Toys created with an imagination, yet absent in developing one.

Geppetto's Workshop doesn't sell these toys. They believe a toy should do more than entertain a child. A toy should spark the creativity that lies within every child.

With this goal in mind, Geppetto's stands by one uncompromising rule: No plastic or batteries.

Geppetto's only sells handcrafted toys made with old-world charm:

Marionettes and hand puppets.
Spinning tops and kaleidoscopes.
Wooden puzzles and games.

A healthy imagination is all that's necessary to get these toys to do anything a child can dream of.
No plastic needed. No batteries required.

*Geppetto's Workshop. Unlock your child's creativity.**

Are you beginning to appreciate how
sacrificing opportunity injects believability
into Geppetto's message?

No plastic. No batteries. It doesn't cut
any sharper than that.

Yes, it's tempting to appeal to everyone.
And business owners often feel compelled
to chase after sales. But doing so only
weakens the credibility of your message.

*This ad was written for demonstration purposes only. Tom
Wanek is not employed by or in any way affiliated with
Geppetto's Workshop.

Scion: Intentionally investing to remain obscure

Like money, popularity is a scoreboard of
life.

The varsity quarterback is considered
"cool" and attracts all the girls.
Celebrities are pop-culture icons stalked by
gossip-pumping paparazzi.

Viral YouTube videos reach millions via web sites, blogs and email.

In business, popularity means that you're a market leader. You sell a product or service people want to buy.

So, the goal of any company is to become popular. *Right?*

Well, not so fast.

First, let this rattle around in your noggin': The head honchos at Scion deliberately take steps to ensure their vehicles remain *unpopular.*

Founded in 2003 by Toyota, Scion was created to attract younger car buyers. But Scion doesn't aim to appeal to all 18 - 24 year olds in the market. No, it intentionally targets the oft-ignored outsider.

Scion's mission is to become the official car company of society's outcasts: The weirdos, rebels and geeks.

The company begins by designing its cars to look unusual. (Dare I say ugly?) Scion's xB model is so unbelievably clunky that buyers have nicknamed it the "Toaster." And there's little doubt that Scion's offbeat styling alienates mainstream car buyers.

But offbeat connects with the outsider.

In 2006 – just three years after launch – Scion's sales reached 175,000 vehicles, exceeding projections by nearly 17 percent. At a time when most car companies are losing sales and market share, Scion's business is booming.

But here's the tightrope it must walk: Scion can't feign loyalty to this crowd.

Why?

Because a true outsider *shuns* the mainstream. And impostors are easy to spot. Any self-respecting non-conformist shrieks with horror at the thought of puttering down the street in a "top-selling" sedan. You won't win their loyalty by declaring that we're all just one big bunch of rebels. *Not a chance.*

But Scion is smart. Very smart. The company realizes fame would shatter its authentic connection with the non-conformist. And, Scion invests opportunity to boost its credibility with the outsider crowd.

Here's Scion's game-plan: In an effort to remain obscure, the company responded to record sales by *lowering* its 2007 production to 150,000 vehicles.

That's not all. Automotive market research firm, Auto Pacifica, reports that the demand for Scion vehicles is enormous. It estimates that Scion could sell up to 250,000 vehicles per year. That's 100,000 units over Scion's 2007 scheduled production!

Here's the financial translation: Conservatively, let's assume the average price of a Scion vehicle is $15,000. Multiply this figure by the 100,000 units and Scion intentionally forfeits *an additional $1.5 billion dollars in gross revenue.*

Let that sink in for a moment.

Most companies would dive into a pool of rusty tacks for $1.5 billion dollars in sales. And let's not forget about Scion's lost opportunities in cash flow, inventory turn and production efficiencies.

Scion's efforts to bypass opportunity don't end there. The company is diligent in their dedication to remain under the radar. Once MySpace.com exploded with popularity, Scion yanked its advertising and moved it to underground online communities such as GaiaOnline.com and Want2BSquare.com

Sacrificing opportunity takes courage.

Scion refuses to become a "corporate sellout" to sell more cars. By intentionally bypassing opportunity, Scion connects with the outsider and expresses a shared identity.

To connect more credibly with your customers, what opportunities are you willing to lose?

Nearly all men can stand adversity, but if you want to test a man's character, give him power.

— Abraham Lincoln

Chapter Seven
Currency: Power & Control

No better words drive home the importance of investing *Power and Control* to signal authenticity and transparency than those crafted by Levine, Locke, Searls and Weinberger in their book, *The Cluetrain Manifesto.*

"A powerful global conversation has begun. Through the Internet, people are discovering and inventing new ways to share relevant knowledge with blinding speed. As a direct result, markets are getting smarter, and getting smarter faster than most companies.

These markets are conversations. Their members communicate in language that is natural, open, honest, direct, funny and often shocking. Whether explaining or

complaining, joking or serious, the human
voice is unmistakably genuine. It can't be
faked.

Most corporations, on the other hand, only
know how to talk in the soothing,
humorless monotone of the mission
statement, marketing brochure, and
your-call-is-important-to-us busy signal.
Same old tone, same old lies. No
wonder networked markets have no respect
for companies unable or unwilling
to speak as they do.

But learning to speak in a human voice
is not some trick, nor will corporations
convince us they are human with lip
service about "listening to customers."
They will only sound human when they
empower real human beings to speak on
their behalf.

While many such people already work for
companies today, most companies ignore

their ability to deliver genuine knowledge, opting instead to crank out sterile happy-talk that insults the intelligence of markets literally too smart to buy it."

Shoeline.com: Revealing an uncomfortable truth.

Are you willing to stand naked in front of your customers?

Most business owners simply don't have the courage. Conventional wisdom tells them to envelop their companies in a shroud of secrecy to prevent the public from uncovering any uncomfortable truths. You know, those stomach-twisting secrets that might cause customers to bolt for the nearest competitor: Drawbacks to a product offering. Gaps in knowledge or expertise. Shortcomings and oversights in service.

To further mask their vulnerabilities and insecurities, business owners project a slick and polished image of infallibility. And this controlling behavior breeds the habitual corporate-speak, hype and chest-thumping clichés that consumers have come to loathe and reject.

But Shoeline.com bucks conventional wisdom by having the courage to reveal an uncomfortable truth: The return history for each and every product it sells. *A decision that has a direct and positive impact on their top-line sales.*

Inspired by Amazon.com's transparency-pioneering customer ratings and reviews, Shoeline.com invented the Return-O-Meter.

The Return-O-Meter is a visual display – similar to an odometer – that indicates how often a particular style of footwear has been returned. And given enough statistical feedback from customers, it will

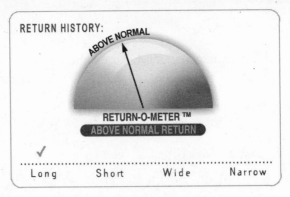

also give the reason for the return – such as a fit that runs too narrow or too wide.

Most retailers cringe at the thought of revealing their product return rates, thinking, "Why in the world would we embarrass ourselves?"

The answer: Because transparency boosts credibility and elevates trust. By admitting the drawbacks, you elevate the believability of the merits.

And gaining trust – especially online – is critical to persuading customers to buy from you. Giving customers better information boosts their buying confidence. Not to mention it's a breath-of-fresh-air.

And I promise you, Shoeline's customers don't think less of them for revealing their warts. They love them for it.

But just how profitable was this investment of power and control for Shoeline.com?

Sales increased by 26 percent.

There's not a retailer on the planet that wouldn't want a 26% increase in sales by investing so little. But would it surprise you to learn that Shoeline.com can do even better?

In the words of my partner Roy H. Williams, "Specifics are more powerful than generalities." I predict Shoeline. com's sales conversions would have increased by at least 50 percent had they gone even further by showing the exact sales numbers and the return rates as a percentage. I would also recommend they define each category on their "Return-O-Meter."   For example, let's say a product's return rate is classified as "Normal" if the number of returns is between 2 - 4 percent of sales.

One last thought: Please don't handcuff your thinking simply because you're not selling online or you are a service provider. Every business or organization can invest *Power and Control.* Begin by looking at what you are keeping from your customers. Have the courage to stand naked.

Google: What signals are you sending to your employees?

Live the pampered life. Captivate your taste buds with rack of lamb or red beet ravioli with tarragon, cashew filling and yellow pepper puree. Restore harmony between mind, body and soul with a workout from a personal trainer, deep tissue massage or stress-busting meditation. Stoke your swagger and style with a shampoo and cut at the hair salon.

Ah, the lifestyle of the rich and famous.

Well, not quite. Get this: These are some of the everyday perks available to Google employees.

Yes, Google.

In 2008, Google clobbered all other corporate giants to top Fortune magazine's list of 100 Best Companies to Work For. A feat the company achieved – for the second year in a row – by investing material wealth to create employee benefits and perks that make working for the tech giant feel less like the daily office grind and more like a a five-star Caribbean vacation.

But look beyond pay and perks, and you'll uncover a more powerful message Google intentionally sends to job seekers and employees alike: a free-spirited and creative culture inspires people to thrive. By giving up the currency of power and control, Google communicates a message perfectly aligned with its corporate motto: "Don't be evil."

And it's shocking to learn just how much freedom Google gives their employees.

Got a whacky idea? Go ahead and run with it. Google allows employees to spend up to 20 percent of their work week – one full day – on a project of their choosing.

Want to ditch the corporate clown suit? Not a problem. Wear your pajamas to work – *if you dare.*

Worried your dog might be lonely sitting at home while you're plugging away at work? Bring your pooch to the office with you. Google loves pets.

No time to finish those nagging chores?
No worries. Get them done during
office hours. Google has on-site doctors,
dentists, massage therapists, hair stylists,
fitness centers, dry cleaning, oil change,
car wash and bike repair. How convenient
is that?

Imprisoned by a lifeless cubical? Liberate
yourself with self-expression. Google
encourages employees to personalize their
work space with decorations, toys and
games.

Yes, Google goes all-out to nurture a fun
and relaxed corporate culture.

But exactly how does this help the
company's bottom-line?

It's simple. Google cultivates innovation
and ingenuity by shoving aside those stuffy
and stale corporate rituals, traditions,
attitudes and beliefs. And doing so helps

the company dominate the competitive, high-speed world of Internet technology and software development. Without it, Google's growth and dominance would quickly fizzle.

Not surprisingly, having the world's cushiest workplace also means that Google is at the top of every job seeker's wish list. And it shows. The company receives more than one-million job applications per year. A nice problem to have if it's critical that you attract and retain top talent.

So how might you invest power and control to motivate staff and grow your company?

The risk of insult is the price of clarity.
- Roy H. Williams

Chapter Eight
Currency: Reputation & Prestige

Patagonia: Love Us or Leave Us
Yvon Chouinard is a maverick. Gritty.
Courageous. Shrewd.

Equally determined, the founder of
outdoor clothing company, Patagonia,
allows *nothing* to stand in his way. And
Chouinard places his love for the outdoors
above all else. *Even above the desires of his
loyal customers.*

Patagonia's roots were planted in
1957 when Chouinard, a world-class
mountaineer, became dissatisfied with
the quality of the climbing equipment
available. As a result, Chouinard taught
himself blacksmithing and began
manufacturing his own equipment,
selling it to climbers he met along the

trail. And by 1972,
Patagonia had evolved
into a manufacturer and
retailer of premium
outdoor clothing.

Fast forward to the
late 1980s: Patagonia
swelled into a corporate
juggernaut with annual
growth accelerating at
40 - 50 percent.

The company was fueled
by a rich and diverse
customer base: The hard-
core outdoorsman swore
by the dependability
of Patagonia clothing.
While the yuppie crowd
donned Patagonia as a
status-symbol.

Patagonia had finally
reached cross-over

appeal. And the company's currency of reputation and prestige was beaming.

But the U.S. recession of 1990 caused a cosmic shift in the mind of Chouinard. Although annual growth still hovered around 20 percent, the economic slowdown caused Chouinard to question Patagonia's strategy of uncontrolled growth. He began researching the environmental impact of manufacturing and – in a heart-stopping moment – was shocked to learn that his own company was destructive.

Chouinard responded with bold and sweeping changes.

His prime directive: Transform Patagonia from a premium outfitter into a champion for the environment. The manufacturing and retailing of Patagonia clothing would simply become the vehicle used to transmit Chouinard's message of environmental sustainability. And his first order of business was to switch Patagonia's cotton clothing from conventional to 100% organic cotton.

Sounds like a snap-your-fingers-and-presto done deal, right?

Not a chance. Back in the environmentalism dark ages of 1993, this was a beastly undertaking. None of the world's major manufacturers or retailers produced cotton clothing made exclusively from organic fibers. Not Levi's. Not Nike. And, most certainly, not Wal-Mart.

Patagonia became the first.

But every revolution is accompanied by protest and push-back from the establishment. Employees grumbled. Suppliers defected. Money bled.

Undeterred, Chouinard marched on. He sent a clear and direct warning to suppliers, "Switch to organic cotton or Patagonia will never use cotton again."

But there was one, not-so-little snag: None of the world's cotton suppliers were equipped to manufacture the amount of organic cotton Patagonia would need. To get the job done, Patagonia had to retool suppliers *at its own expense*. And the decision to go organic *doubled* the price of cotton.

The once vibrant Patagonia now struggled to earn a profit.

Now here's where things get super dicey: Patagonia risked its reputation and prestige with its loyal customers when the company began preaching and practicing environmental sustainability at the retail level.

Chouinard carved out *forty-five percent* of the company's recurring retail catalog space to offer instructions on how one can better live in harmony with the environment. The company also mandates that shoppers refrain from wasteful purchases: Patagonia doesn't want you to buy from them unless the items are absolutely needed. And overnight delivery is heavily discouraged. Expedited shipping equals wasted fuel.

Patagonia also discontinued many popular products that couldn't be manufactured in an eco-friendly way. This obsessive purging of products is a tradition the company still practices today – even though customers find it aggravating.

Not surprisingly, more than 50 percent of Patagonia's correspondence comes from disgruntled customers. Here's one such customer who found her organic undies in a bunch over Patagonia's "Vote for the Environment" campaign:

"We are given the gift of our land by God in which to have dominion. That means to use and to a degree pollute. We are also called by God not to worship idols. The notion of a largely untouched pristine environment has become a quasi-religious idol for many. Hence with regard to environmentalism we have a distorted hubris, even dark influence."

You have to build a thick wall to remain standing under a barrage of scathing remarks. But in true maverick fashion, Chouinard stays the course and takes a "love us or leave us" attitude.

Here's Chouinard's response to this customer's caustic comments and concerns:

"It's surprising, not alarming. I couldn't care less. I could get 10,000 letters

saying "Take me off your mailing list"
and it wouldn't bother me. If you're not
getting those letters, you're not trying hard
enough. That's the way I see it. What
they don't realize is that I'm not in the
business to make clothes. I'm not in the
business to make more money for myself,
for Christ's sakes. This is the reason
Patagonia exists – to put into action the
recommendations I read about in books
to avoid environmental collapse. That's
the reason I'm in business – to try to clean
up our own act, and try to influence other
companies to do the right thing, and try
to influence our customers to do the right
thing. So we're not going to change. They
can go buy from somewhere else if they
don't like it."

Now, it's shockingly clear that by risking
its reputation and prestige, Patagonia's
message of environmental responsibility
is believable. No one would question

the company's sincerity or mistake this statement as hyperbole.

But, does Patagonia's message unite customers with the company or disconnect them from it?

The answer is both. And I specifically shared the example for this very reason.

The outdoor aficionados – who worship nature and care about conservation every bit as much as Chouinard – believe Patagonia's values are aligned with their own. *And, they're obviously right.*

However, those trendy little twits – wearing Patagonia as a status symbol, and whose idea of roughing it in the great outdoors is cutting the lawn – now see a chasm between the values of Patagonia and their own. *And, they're correct, too.*

They can't begin to comprehend why Patagonia would risk its good name by flinging this strict environmental spiel onto its customers.

Knowing this will help you appreciate that one's perceptual reality shapes the meaning of every message. And not everyone will share the same interpretation.

But don't sweat it. Remember, you're not going to arm-twist everyone into buying from you. *So please don't try.*

Patagonia didn't try. Instead, the company risked its stellar reputation and prestige when Chouinard redefined its values. And, in every instance where Patagonia placed the environment over the perceived happiness of its customers, the company was rewarded with a sustained leap in sales and a deeper commitment from its army of outdoor-loving shoppers.

Today, Patagonia remains a privately held company with annual sales exceeding $270 million dollars.

Avis: Throwing down its reputation and prestige

Your company's reputation is a lifeline to credibility. You cannot become or remain successful without one. And as a general rule, it's reckless to risk one's good name.

But in 1962, Avis bucked conventional wisdom and placed its reputation on a tightrope with its legendary, "We Try Harder" campaign. A bold move that boomed Avis' credibility and sparked spectacular growth.

Here's how it all went down: After 13 consecutive years of operating in the red, Avis found itself nearly bankrupt. The company sucked wind trying to catch up to juggernaut Hertz. In a last-ditch effort,

Avis sought to hire an ad agency with enough mojo to keep the company from circling the drain.

But most heavyweight ad agencies turned Avis away. Few wanted to take a chance on an unprofitable company with lousy service and a crappy product. Only advertising legend Bill Bernbach and his firm Doyle Dane and Bernbach (DDB) accepted the challenge.

But Bernbach was no fool. His firm would sign-on only if Avis agreed to two unwavering conditions.

First, DDB insisted Avis upgrade their product and service. Sparkling cars. Hydrated gas tanks. Sunny dispositions and glowing smiles. Bernbach's reasoning:

"It's always a mistake to make good advertising for a bad product."

Finally, DDB also demanded full authority over the ad campaign. No objections. No compromises. No modifications. And in his line-in-the-sand moment, Bernbach informed Avis CEO Bob Townsend, "You must promise to run everything we write, without changing a bloody comma."

The outcome: Advertising history. The epic "We Try Harder" campaign became one heck of a meal ticket. Avis pulled a u-turn and was profitable within a year. And by 1966, the company rose from 10% market share to a whopping 35 percent. *Now that's darn impressive.*

But allow me to make this crystal clear: Any company can claim to try harder. And many do. Yes, making powerful statements is easy. But making these statements *believable* is not so easy.

Avis' power statement brimmed with believability.

Here's why: As you might recall, the credibility linchpin for the entire strategy was revealing Avis' position as the #2 car rental company in the industry. And Avis' credibility boost was directly related to the company's willingness to invest-its reputation and prestige.

Without this bold and unprecedented admission, the "We Try Harder" slogan would have been nothing more than a limp, unsubstantiated claim. (Can you say advertising bomb?)

Avis can't afford dirty ashtrays.

Or to start you out without a full gas tank, a new car like a lively, super-torque Ford, a smile.
Why?
When you're not the biggest in rent a cars, you have to try harder.
We do.
We're only No. 2.

No. 2ism. The Avis Manifesto.

We are in the rent a car business, playing second fiddle to a giant.
Above all, we've had to learn how to stay alive.
In the struggle, we've also learned the basic difference between the No. 1's and No. 2's of the world.
The No. 1 attitude is: "Don't do the wrong thing. Don't make mistakes and you'll be O.K."
The No. 2 attitude is: "Do the right thing. Look for new ways. Try harder."
No. 2ism is the Avis doctrine. And it works.
The Avis customer rents a clean, new Opel Rekord, with wipers wiping, ashtrays empty, gas tank full, from an Avis girl with smile firmly in place.
And Avis itself has come out of the red into the black.
Avis didn't invent No. 2ism. Anyone is free to use it.
No. 2's of the world, arise!

And man, oh man was this confession controversial. Avis executives flipped when they polled the public only to discover that fifty-percent would perceive the company as being second-rate. But Bernbach was fearless. He knew that the remaining half represented more than enough customers to grow Avis' business. And, he was right.

Said DDB copywriter, Paula Green, "It almost didn't run. Everything was against it. It was a thorny ad. It wasn't pretty. It printed unprintable truths. It exposed the naked company to the public. It made a lot of people uncomfortable. It even irritated a lot of people at DDB. It researched miserably. Bill Bernbach had the courage to sell it."

This is another example of Roy H. William's Law of Polarity from Chapter Six: "Your business' ability to attract customers cannot exceed its potential to repel."

Surprisingly, Avis still advertises the "We try harder" slogan today. But it doesn't have the zip and zing as it once did. *Not even close.*

Why?

Because Avis stopped risking reputation and prestige when it dropped the "We're #2" piece of the strategy. And with it, went all credibility.

Currently, Avis trails market leader Enterprise. The company knows that it's impossible to convince the public you're trying hard enough when, after nearly five decades of effort, you're still number two. It requires a suspension of disbelief. And this isn't the movies. It's time for Avis to adopt a new strategy.

Remember that signaling is only convincing when you stay true to yourself.

Just as weak and inferior gazelles do not stot, if you can't support what you're signaling, then don't send that particular signal. Redirect your resources.

Take calculated risks. That is quite different from being rash.

— George S. Patton

Chapter Nine
Currency: Safety & Well-Being

LifeLock: Betting the farm with nine, tiny little digits

Your personal identity is under siege: Social Security number. Bank accounts. Credit cards.

Are you prepared?

Identity theft now edges out drug trafficking as the fastest growing crime in the United States. Nearly 10 million Americans have their identities stolen each year. And in 2008, identity thieves – cloaked by a digital veil – snatched an estimated $48 billion dollars from victims.

Today's technology connects the world and gives us instant access to information – largely a godsend. But this connectivity and access is interwoven with rushing darkness and crime. The Internet has become a holy grail for scam artists, hackers and thieves. In early 2009, colossal data breaches affecting Monster.com and Heartland Payment Systems have put tens of millions of people at potential risk of identity theft.

What a nightmare. But this growing plague provided a glowing opportunity for LifeLock – a company started in 2005 to protect the personal identity of consumers.

Here's a run-down on Lifelock's identity-theft protection service: For a $10 monthly fee, LifeLock places your credit file on "fraud alert" with the major credit bureaus (Equifax, Experian and TransUnion). This alert is a safeguard requiring lenders to verify your identify – by calling the phone number you designate – before any credit can be issued under your name.

Fraud alerts are temporary, expiring every 90-days. LifeLock automatically renews this alert as a part of its service.

The company's efforts to protect your identity also include removing your name from pre-approved offers for insurance and credit cards, sending yearly free credit reports from the major credit bureaus, and helping you cancel your accounts and replace these items should your wallet ever go missing. The service also continuously scours the Internet and nationwide address databases for any illegal activity using your personal information.

Given the circumstances, one might imagine that Lifelock would have transformed into an on-the-spot success.

But that didn't happen.

Even in a world swarming with fraud, Lifelock found it difficult to gain traction.

The company had no perceived reputation
to speak of, and was hindered by marketing
a subject that conjures up an unpleasant
mental image in the public's mind.

But this didn't deter Lifelock. With
nine, tiny little digits the company risks
safety and well-being to demonstrate the
effectiveness of its service.

Here's how: LifeLock CEO, Todd Davis,
brazenly dares thieves to steal his personal
identity by running ads that say, *"My name
is Todd Davis. My social security number
is 457-55-5462. So why publish my social*

security number? Because I'm absolutely
confident LifeLock is protecting my good name
and personal information, just like it will
yours. And we guarantee our service up to $1
million dollars."

Pretty darn convincing, huh?

Admittedly, this attention-grabbing
demonstration borders on being gimmicky.
But Lifelock's strategy is persuasive
because it's anchored in relevancy. The
company knows that a message absent
of relevancy is equivalent to falsely
screaming fire in a crowded theater. It will
not persuade.

Todd Davis offers unmistakable proof
that Lifelock will protect your personal
identity. He risks his personal safety and
well-being through the publication of his
Social Security number and also risks his
company's material wealth by reimbursing
up to $1 million in identity-theft losses.

This strategy to invest currencies to buy credibility has built Lifelock into the dominant player in its category.

Concorde: Demonstrating Confidence in the Plane's Safety

At sixty-thousand feet, the sky darkens and the curvature of the Earth is revealed as you dance with the edge of space.

Concorde took you there.

No other aircraft captivated the public's fascination like Concorde. In supersonic flight, the jet travelled at twice the speed of sound. Zipping across the Atlantic in 2 hours and 53 minutes. New York to Paris in half the time of a typical, subsonic commercial flight.

Sadly, like a Hollywood star that dies too young, Concorde experienced a tragic ending.

In his Monday Morning Memo titled,
"Time and Chance," dated December
28th, 2007, Roy H. Williams recounts
Concorde's demise:

*"During a routine take-off in July, 2000, Concorde
blew a tire after hitting a small piece of metal on a
runway in Paris. A chunk of the tire knocked a hole
in the wing, spilling fuel down the side of the plane
just as it was lifting off. Ninety seconds later, the
plane exploded in the air. The public was terrified.*

*The Concorde fleet
was grounded. After
reinforcing the wings
with bulletproof Kevlar and
installing puncture-proof tires,
the senior executives of Concorde's
parent company boarded the plane in September,
2001 and flew halfway across the Atlantic and
back to demonstrate their confidence in the plane's
safety. While they were in the air, terrorists flew
commercial jets into the World Trade Center. Now
everyone was afraid to travel.*

*Having already been out of operation for 14
months, Concorde was unable to recover from this
second financial whammy."*

Now let there be no doubt: The decision to have Concorde senior executives risk their own safety and well-being to demonstrate the plane's safety was brilliant.
Absolutely brilliant.

What better way to restore the public's rattled confidence?

Sure, the company could have simply pointed out the new safety modifications. And it might have also reminded the public that Concorde had been the world's safest passenger airliner prior to the Paris crash. This approach would have worked for any other airliner.

But this was Concorde.

The jet pushed the boundaries like no other commercial plane could. And words *alone* would not have done enough to diminish the public's anxiety of flying

aboard Concorde. A greater investment
was required.

And yes, I'm absolutely convinced that
had this demonstration occurred on any
other day, Concorde passengers would be
dancing with the edge of space still today.

Part Three:
Tying It Altogether

The search for signs of trustworthiness makes us into mind readers, alert for any twitch of inconsistency that betrays a sham.

    - Stephen Pinker, *How the Mind Works*

Chapter Ten
The Three Questions of Message Alignment

Communication is powerful when actions and words agree. And just as it has for many of the companies we've reviewed, investing currencies can boom your credibility and make you top dog in your category:

> Jim Gilbert's Wheels and Deals backing up the reliability of its vehicles by giving each one a rigorous inspection along with a no-cost, 6-month/12,000 kilometer warranty.

> One Hour Heating and Air Conditioning guaranteeing on-time arrival for service calls or you don't owe them a dime.

Lifelock's CEO demonstrating his company's ability to protect your personal identity against theft by publishing his real Social Security number.

But as we've also learned from the Sprint example, nothing will erode your credibility faster than conflict between what you are saying and who you are being. The brain immediately recognizes any inconsistencies, and reacts by raising a bright red flag of disconnect and doubt. So cheap talk won't win your customer's loyalty or trust. *Period.*

But inconsistencies sometimes creep up unintentionally. And these things happen to the best of us. Therefore, there are three straightforward questions that business owners and marketers should ask themselves regularly to ensure their actions and words agree.

The Three Questions of Message Alignment:

1. What are your company's defining characteristics?

What makes your business special? What are those values that your business stands for, or against? What promises or claims are being made in your advertising? How about on your website? And don't forget about the unspoken expectations customers might have of you. *Be diligent. Flush everything out.*

2. What signals do your decisions send?

Look at your business through the eyes of the customer. Start with the basics: Review your hours-of-operation. Comb through your policies and procedures. Examine the decisions that your employees make. And most importantly, gather customer feedback, comments and reviews of your products or services.

Google Alerts is a crafty way to keep tabs on your company's reputation. This free service allows you to choose multiple keywords that are relevant to your business. Google will then scour the Internet and email you each time any of these words have been mentioned relative to to your company. *Pretty powerful stuff, huh?*

3. Is there conflict between what you are saying and who you are being?

Remember, your company's credibility is at stake here. Move quickly to reconcile any contradiction: Whack the clichés. Close all loopholes. Substantiate every claim. Investigate any complaint or concern.

Now, let's apply these three questions and learn how Toyota recognized and resolved a major conflict in their message.

Toyota:
The Worlds "Greenest" Automaker

Over the years, Toyota has cultivated several defining characteristics that have made it the world's largest automaker:

Unmatched reliability.
Responsiveness to market demands.
Sleek and attractive cars.

But their latest endeavor is to become the world's "greenest" automaker. (Answering our first question of message alignment – a company's defining characteristics.)

And why not? Toyota already has a significant head start.

The Prius – Toyota's best-selling, hybrid-only model – commands 51 percent of the hybrid market. And in fall 2007, Toyota began advertising its harmonious relationship with the environment by stating the company's goal of "striving for zero waste in everything else we do."

Sounds pretty responsible, right?

Well, not so fast. Before we crown Toyota king of the environmental hill, let's look closer at some of the decisions the company has made, and consider what its actions might be signaling. (Our second question of message alignment.)

An October 3rd, 2007 New York Times article, *"Et Tu Toyota,"* reported that Toyota has joined forces with the Big Three U.S. automakers in lobbying *against* improved U.S. mileage standards outlined in the Senate's draft of a new energy bill.

Lobbing *against* tougher milage standards?

Now hold on. One expects the world's "greenest" automaker to be in favor of improving fuel economy – not against it. And if it really gave a hoot about the environment, Toyota would be leading the charge to raise milage standards.

But that's not all. In yet another credibility misstep, *The Associated Press* reported on November 14th 2007 that "Toyota faces questions about quality, environment at Los Angeles Auto Show."

So what caused the big hubbub at the Los Angeles Auto Show?

Toyota's debut of the Sequoia – its redesigned, full-size SUV. *Yes, Toyota's show-stopping announcement was a gas-guzzler.*

Allow me to remind you that California is the nation's most environmentally-friendly state. And for months, Californians have been dazzled by ads promoting Toyota's message of sustainability.

So is there conflict between what Toyota is saying and who they are being? (Our third question of message alignment.)

You bet there is. And it's undeniable.

But Toyota recognized this conflict and reacted quickly to realign its actions and words.

Returning to its message of sustainability, Toyota rolled into Detroit's 2008 North American International Auto Show – the world's premier auto event – debuting the A-BAT, the company's new **hybird** compact pick-up. *An auto-industry first.*

Now here's why this is a big deal: The Sequoia is currently in mass production. And the vehicle is a huge moneymaker for Toyota. But the A-BAT is a concept car that might never reach mass production.

To help it sell more cars *today,* Toyota would prefer nothing more than to place the Sequoia in the spotlight. But the company sacrifices this opportunity to realign its actions and words, and regain its credibility.

How might you do the same?

The whole is greater than the sum of its parts.
                                        - Gestalt Theory

Chapter 11
The Anatomy of a Power Statement

Credibility is a vital part of persuasive communication. Without it, your message will be unremarkable and unconvincing. And as we've discovered, investing one or more of the six currencies injects your marketing message with a strong dose of credibility, which leads consumers to *anticipate* a trustworthy buying experience.

But before you go happily humming along looking to invest currencies for your own business, just know that projecting credibility, alone, is not enough. It is but one part of the larger body of persuasive communication. And for marketers, that body of communication is a company's *power statement.*

A power statement is a marketing message consisting of three essential persuasive parts: relevancy, contrasting and credibility.

Now you might think that a power statement is like those superficial positioning statements of the past – the ones marketers celebrate and hang on the office wall.

It most certainly is not.

Persuasive communication cannot be the result of a one-size-fits-all formula that spits out an all-encompassing declaration of how you *hope* to be perceived.

Yes, a power statement provides a framework that encompasses your company's marketing message, and serves as a guideline from which all advertising should be based. But a power statement also has real persuasive teeth, applying principles borrowed from biology, neurology and psychology.

As an expression of your business that goes beyond words, a power statement's goal is to eliminate any ambiguity or doubt about what your product or service will do for the customer. No hoopla. No fanfare. No wall-hanging ceremonies.

So now that we've set the record straight, let's dissect the three main elements of a power statement and learn where investing currencies fits into the entire mechanism of persuasive marketing communication.

Relevancy: What is it that you do and why should I care?

Persuasive communication demands relevancy. Which means your marketing message must communicate an idea, feeling or outcome that the customer truly cares about.

And here's what is critical: Your message should not revolve around you or your company. It should focus on the customer. Specifically, your marketing message must explain what your product or service will do for the customer. Get this part wrong and nothing else matters.

So keeping our case studies handy, let's zip through a few sparkling examples:

- REI speaks to the novice searching for reliable expertise and equipment in preparation for a rigorous outdoor adventure.
- Scion speaks to the outsider rejecting mainstream society who wishes to express a non-conformist attitude by driving a car that's a little bit offbeat.
- Geppetto's Workshop speaks to the belief that a toy should foster a child's imagination.
- Patagonia speaks to the outdoor enthusiast who wants to live in better harmony with the environment by wearing eco-friendly clothing.

So what is the felt need of *your* customer that you are willing and able to meet?

Not sure where to begin?

Start by uncovering those questions customers ask most often about your business, products or services. These frequently asked questions will also clue you in on any uncertainty customers might have about buying from you.

But don't grapple with this question all on your own. Tap into the knowledge and experience of your front-line employees. Staff members in direct, daily contact with your customers will likely provide an eye-opening perspective and move you imminently closer to uncovering your customer's felt need.

Still, the search for your customer's true motivation to buy might elude you or otherwise lie off the beaten path. In this case, look beyond the customer's primary need and zero in on a complementary need.

Consider that a car buyer doesn't purchase a BMW simply as a means of transportation. No, a used Honda Civic sufficiently gets you around town. *BMW has become a status symbol.* And the motivation to buy the "Ultimate Driving Machine®" – the customer's felt need – comes from the desire to signal one's wealth or success.

Also recall that One Hour Heating and Air Conditioning bypassed the customer's primary need of heating or cooling their home, and instead made saving the customer's time its top priority.

Are you beginning to appreciate the importance of communicating a relevant message?

Speaking to the customer's felt need – that
which is relevant – is the heart of a power
statement. And powerful statements
always speak to the customer's felt need.
I repeat, always.

Contrasting: Framing the customer's buying experience

The Contrast Principle in psychology
states that decisions are not made
in isolation. Rather, we look for the
differences among our available options.

Contrasting in marketing is the degree
to which your message strikes a clear and
unmistakable difference between you and
your competition. And as a marketer, it's
your job to frame the buying scenario for
the consumer. The objective is to clearly
state what your product or service does
and why this makes you the obvious choice.

Begin by listing the defining characteristics
of your business and those of the buying

alternative. Give plenty of details. (Now is not the time to hold back.) Contrasting is only effective when you use specifics not generalities. And, the first company – competing in a given market – to successfully define their position and that of the competition typically wins the game.

Want an example of contrasting in action?

Ask and ye shall receive. Take a gander at the following copy for 5-Hour Energy:

A typical energy drink comes with a lot of extra baggage – 12 teaspoons of sugar, 200 calories, herbal stimulants and 16 ounces of fluid. This combination can make you feel wired up then let you down with a crash. So don't drink energy drinks. Drink a 5-Hour Energy shot. It has zero sugar, zero herbal stimulants and as much caffeine as a cup of the leading premium coffee. And best of all – only four little calories. - Source: http://www.5hourenergy.com/

Using 77 words – the approximate length of a 30-second ad – 5-Hour Energy clearly contrasts the difference between their energy shot and those "canned" energy drinks swimming in calories and sugar. And notice the impressive amount of details:

Typical energy drink:
- 12 teaspoons of sugar
- 200 calories
- Herbal stimulants and 16 ounces of fluid

5-Hour Energy shot:
- Zero sugar
- Zero herbal stimulants
- As much caffeine as a cup of the leading premium coffee

The added whammy is the natural language and conversational tone used in the copy. Words like, "extra baggage" and "wired up" provide a clean break from the ho-hum clichés one typically finds in marketing and advertising.

5-Hour Energy contrasts brilliantly, but Post Shredded Wheat is equally effective at this technique while taking a slightly different approach. Rather than contrasting against competing cereal brands, Post Shredded Wheat contrasts against the idea of progress and innovation:

Progress is Overrated

Has progress taken us to a better place?

I'd say it's taken us for a ride. (Probably in a carbon-coughing oil guzzler.)

Honestly, what thanks do we owe progress? We're up to our necks in landfill, down to the wire on resources, and climate change is out to get us - or at best leave us with a nasty sunburn.

Historically, civilizations are destroyed by progress. Just ask the Pharaohs. No sooner had they built those jumbo triangles and giant cement cats than they flushed themselves down the Nile.

That's why at Post Shredded Wheat, we put the "no" in innovation.

Henry Perky created the Original Shredded Wheat in 1892. One man. (Him.) On ingredient. (Wheat.) One machine. (The machine.) We didn't give it any add-ons or plug-ins. Heck, we didn't even name it.

All we did was make it Spoon Size in 1961. Did we go too far? Time will tell. But I will say our naturally fiber-rich, 100% whole grain wheat has been free of enhancement, progress and pyramids for 117 years and counting.

Frank Druffel

So here's the bottom line: Both 5-Hour Energy and Post Shredded Wheat successfully use contrasting to position their products and provide consumers with concrete, compelling reasons to buy from them. No lingering questions. No branding campaigns using silly mascots. No attempts to dazzle you with baloney and hype.

Give your customers this same type of clarity. They're craving it.

Credibility: What are you willing to risk or spend?

Like it or not, your customers are looking for a buying experience they can trust. Consider that five thousand advertising messages ambush us daily. And many of these ads are overloaded with ad-speak and hype, leaving overwhelmed consumers scrambling to decipher which messages are believable.

To that end, the majority of this book has been focused on learning how to inject credibility into your marketing by investing one or more of six currencies:

1. Material Wealth
2. Time & Energy
3. Opportunity
4. Power & Control
5. Reputation & Prestige
6. Safety & Well-Being

So which currency will you risk or spend to buy credibility?

Need a refresher? Rather than rehash the principles here, go back and dive into the case studies in Part Two of this book. There, you'll find plenty of ideas and inspiration to apply to your own business.

Putting it all together:

The sweet spot for any marketing message is synchronizing the three main elements of a power statement. To maximize persuasive impact, they must reinforce one another.

For example, let's say we're marketing a tech company whose primary business is providing IT support to small and medium-sized companies in a single geographic location.

Here's what the power statement's three elements might look like:

Relevancy (the customer's felt need): To spend time where it truly counts – running their business – instead of dealing with the ongoing hassle of IT support.

Contrasting: Tech Wizards is a full-service IT support company that's available 24/7. And you can always reach a live person. We're not some telephone or cable conglomerate that's challenging to access when you need IT support.

Credibility investment: Power and control. Demonstrating Tech Wizards' availability by publishing the company president's cell phone number.

See how this works? And notice that continuity exists between all three persuasive elements. The power statement starts by addressing the customer's felt need, which is to remove the headache of IT support and allow the business owner to concentrate on growing the company. Then, both contrasting and the credibility investment reinforce this need by demonstrating the availability and responsiveness of Tech Wizards' IT support.

That was easy. Now let's take this power statement and turn it into polished ad copy:

Your business isn't running as smoothly as it should.

It just can't when you're monkeying around with the latest tech thingamajig, that web whatchamacallit and those domain doohickies. After all, your time is better spent growing your business – not dealing with the extra baggage of running an in-house IT department.

Turn your technology needs over to Tech Wizards.

Hi, I'm Doug Smith, president of Tech Wizards. We're Northeast Ohio's full-service IT support company – not some overstuffed telephone or cable conglomerate that won't be there when you need them. We handle:

- *Support desk staffing*
- *Hardware installation*
- *Network security*

When it comes to IT support, Tech Wizards can run the whole kit and caboodle. And you can always speak to a live person whenever you need us. In fact, you can even reach me on my cell at 555-555-5555. Yes, that's my direct line. And there's not a single administrative assistant to protect me. As I said, we're always there for you. So let Tech Wizards handle your IT needs, and get back to growing your business.

As you can see from our fictional company, the one thing you won't find with a power statement is quiet, understated ad copy. A power statement produces copy that is direct and persuasive. But it requires a marketer that has the courage to break from the norm.

Do you have what it takes?

Do you have a quiet ferocity? Are you willing to take a chance? Will you throw your cap over the wall, kill the ox and burn the plow, run toward the sound of the guns?

— Roy H. Williams

Chapter 12
Final Thoughts

Throughout this book I've argued that your customers are looking for a buying experience they can trust. And because the mind weighs the cost associated with one's actions, you can purchase credibility by investing one or more of six currencies.

But for a moment, put aside the fact that investing currencies works as a persuasive tool. Instead, focus on the internal challenges you'll face with implementing such a strategy.

Like your customers, you are guided by a nervous system that is programmed to avoid risk and the pain of loss. And what you stand to lose or gain from your available choices impacts every decision you make.

Emotion is the driving force used by your nervous system to influence your decisions.

Feelings of fear and trepidation are triggered by the unknown. These emotions prompt you to invest your resources cautiously.

Feelings of trust, comfort and security are triggered by things familiar: Family and friends. Ethnic background. Political affiliations.

Humans have long trusted the wisdom of groups as a survival mechanism. Neuroscientist Read Montague explains, "There is, of course, great value in belonging to a group. Safety in numbers, for one. But there is also a mathematical explanation for why the brain is so willing to give up its own opinions: a group of people is more likely to be correct about something than an individual."

In essence, your natural instinct is to follow the herd. And it's counterintuitive for you to risk or spend your own limited resources. Which means you must battle human nature if you wish to purchase credibility for your business.

But buying credibility is exactly what you should do.

Recall from the very beginning of this book, the example of the stotting gazelle. To the outside observer, stotting is a ridiculous behavior. It makes no sense that the gazelle would unnecessarily risk its safety and well-being to stop and leap up and down while facing an advancing cheetah.

But insiders know that stotting makes perfect sense.

For healthy, courageous gazelles, stotting sends a message that it can outrun and

outlast the cheetah. And the fact that
the gazelle squanders precious time and
energy gives this signal a high degree of
believability.

And now, you're an insider.

But you're not out of the thicket just
yet. Keeping your emotions in check
is not enough. Your opinion will likely
be dwarfed by those within your own
organization.

Surely in the weeks or months to come
you're going to hear comments like, "But
a *'No questions asked'* return policy might
backfire. Our returns could skyrocket."
Or, "We should never reveal our mistakes.
What will our customers think?"

Sure, there will always be risks. But
credibility requires an investment that
goes beyond words. And playing it safe is
a deceivingly risky strategy.

Just remember, fear and trepidation is the monster that will prevent you from buying credibility for your business. So have the courage to walk the road less traveled. I'll be cheering you on.

About the Author

Entrepreneurship tugging at his heart, Tom Wanek spent eight years growing his successful retail-clothing store. Dealing with his fair share of growing pains, skinned knees and all. Just like you.

Today, as a Wizard of Ads partner Tom's passion and commitment is helping owner-operated companies in North America and Australia grow their business.

As an adjunct faculty member of the Wizard Academy® in Austin, Texas, he teaches the workshops, "Fight the Big Boys and Win" and "Currencies that Buy Credibility." Tom is an international speaker who enthusiastically shares his pioneering ideas at home and abroad.

Bibliography

Alexander, Christopher and Sara Ishikawa, Murray Silverstein, Max Jacobson, Ingrid Fiksdahl-King, Shlomo Angel. A Pattern Language. New York: Oxford University Press, 1977: 774.

Archer, Michelle. "Founder of Patagonia became a businessman accidently." USA TODAY. 30 October 2005. Web. November 2007. <http://www.usatoday.com/money/books/reviews/2005-10-30-patagonia_x.htm>.

"Avis Rent a Car, Inc." Jiffynotes.com. Web. May 2009. <http://www.jiffynotes.com/a_study_guides/book_notes_add/emmc_0001_0001_0/emmc_0001_0001_0_00031.html>.

"Avis: We Try Harder." BuildingBrands. Web. May 2008. <http:www.buildingbrands.com/didyouknow/16_avis_we_try_harder.php>.

Casey, Susan. "Patagonia: Blueprint for green business." Fortune. 29 May 2007. Web. November 2007. <http://money.cnn.com/magazines/fortune/   fortune_archive/2007/04/02/8403423/index.htm>.

Chon, Gina. "A Way Cool Strategy: Toyota's Scion Plans To Sell Fewer Cars." The Wall Street Journal - WSJ.com. 10 Nov. 2007. Web. December 2008. <http://online.wsj.com/article/SB116313070935919553.html?mod=djemITP>.

Clock Work Home Services, Inc. Web. December 2008. <http://www.clockworkhomeservices.com>.

"Concorde." Wikipedia. Web. April 2009. <http://en.wikipedia.org/wiki/Concorde>.

Concorde SST - The Definitive Concorde Aircraft Site on the Internet. Web. April 2009. <http://www.concordesst.com>.

"Contrast Principle." Changing Minds. Web. May 2009. <http://changingminds.org/principles/contrast.htm>.

Diggins, Brent and Cathy Planchard. "Media Advisory-Expert Insight into the 2008 FTC Identity and Fraud Report." Reuters. 27 February 2009. Web. April 2009. <http://www.reuters.com/article/pressRelease/idUS369284+27-Feb-2009+BW20090227>.

"Doing Well by Doing Good: Why Patagonia Makes a Profit, Naturally." Treehugger. 26 August 2008. Web. November 2007. <http://www.treehugger.com/files/2008/08/doing-well-by-doing-good.php>.

Durbin, Dee-Ann. "Toyota faces questions about quality, environment at Los Angeles Auto Show." The New York Times. 15 November 2007. Web. December 2007. <http://www.nytimes.com/2007/11/15/business/worldbusiness/15iht-toyota.1.8349356.html>.

"Edelman Trust Baromoter 2008." Web. May 2008. <http://www.edelman.co.uk/files/trust-barometer-2008.pdf>. FOXNews.com. "Sprint Hangs Up on High-Maintenance Customers." Web. 09 July 2007. <http://www.foxnews.com/story/0,2933,288635,00.html>.

Friedman, Thomas L. "Et Tu, Toyota?." The New York Times. 03 October 2007. Web. December 2007. <http://www.nytimes.com/2007/10/03/opinion/03friedman.html>.

Griscom Little, Amanda. "Patagonia clothing founder ponders politics, saving Earth." MSNBC.com. 28 October 2004. Web. November 2007. <http://www.msnbc.msn.com/id/6353516/>.

"How Product Return System Lifted Conversions (Surprise) 26%." MarketingSherpa. 03 July 2008. Web. 03 July 2008. <https://www.marketingsherpa.com/barrier.html?ident=30273>.

"Hybrid sales, led by Prius, up 38 percent in '07." MSNBC.com. 21 April 2008. Web. February 2009. <http://www.msnbc.msn.com/id/24230209/>.

"Identity theft hits record 10M Americans." CNNMoney.com. 09 February 2009. Web. April 2009. <http://money.cnn.com/2009/02/09/news/newsmakers/identity_theft.reut/index.htm?postversion=2009020907>.

Jim Gilbert's Wheel's and Deals. Web. 22 January 2008.
<http://www.revup.ca/>.

Jones, Roland. "Under fire, Toyota offers green spin for fleet." MSNBC.
com. 28 November 2007. Web. December 2007.
<http://www.msnbc.msn.com/id/21940503/>.

Kopytoff, Verne. "Study says Google top workplace." SFGate.
09 January 2007. Web. May 2008. <http://www.sfgate.com/cgi-bin/
article.cgi?f=/c/a/2007/01/09/BUGJSNF2171.DTL>.

Levs, Josh. "Big Three auto CEOs flew private jets to ask for taxpayer
money." CNN. 19 November 2008. Web. 19 November 2008.
<http://www.cnn.com/2008/US/11/19/autos.ceo.jets/index.html>.

LifeLock - Identity Theft Prevention. Web. November 2007.
<http://www.lifelock.com>.

Montague, Read. Why Choose This Book. New York: Dutton, 2006.

Morrissey, Brian. "Scion Web Strategy Takes Stealth Approach."
AdWeek. 22 October 2007. Web. November 2007.
<http://www.adweek.com/aw/esearch/article_display.jsp?vnu_
content_id=1003661099>.

Nelson, Robert. "Sprint may cancel your service if you call customer
service too often." Gadgetell. 06 July 2007. Web. November 2007.
<http://www.gadgetell.com/tech/comment/sprint-may-cancel-your-
service-if-you-call-customer-service-to-often/>.

"No Phone for You! Sprint-Nextel Cuts Off High-Maintenance
Customers." Knowledge@W.P. Carey. 29 August 2007. Web. November
2007. <http://knowledge.wpcarey.asu.edu/article.cfm?articleid=1464>.

One Hour Heating and Air Conditioning. Web. December 2007.
<http://www.onehourair.com/>.

"Poor Customer Service is Top Reason Consumers Switch Service
Providers." Cellular-news. 27 July 2005. Web. January 2008.
<http://www.cellular-news.com/story/13560.php>.

Progressive - Auto Insurance Quote: Car & Motorcycle Insurance. Web. August 2007. <http://www.progressive.com>.

Reardon, Marguerite. "Sprint breaks up with high-maintenance customers." CNET News. 05 July 2007. Web. November 2009. <http://news.cnet.com/8301-10784_3-9739869-7.html>.

REI Expert Advice: Outdoor Adventure How To Articles and Videos. Web. 02 October 2007. < http://www.rei.com/expertadvice>.

"Return-O-Meter reduces returns and boosts click-throughs for Shoeline.com." InternetRetailer.com. 19 October 2007 Web. 19 October 2007. <http://www.internetretailer.com/internet/marketing-conference/75143-return-o-meter-reduces-returns-boosts-click-throughs-shoelinecom.html>.

Schneier, Bruce. "The Pros and Cons of LifeLock." Wired. 12 June 2008. Web. April 2009. <http://www.wired.com/politics/security/commentary/securitymatters/2008/06/securitymatters_0612?currentPage=2>.

"Scion xB." Wikipedia. Web. June 2009. <http://en.wikipedia.org/wiki/Scion_xb>.

Second Chance Armor, Inc. Web. 10 February 2008. <http://www.secondchance.com>.

Shoeline.com. Web. December 2008. <http://www.shoeline.com/>.

Smith, John Maynard and David Harper. Animal Signals. New York: Oxford University Press, 2003.

"Sprint Nextel Hires a Chief from Its Spinoff." The New York Times. Web. 10 December 2007. 02 Aug. 2009. <http://www.nytimes.com/2007/12/19/technology/19sprint.html?_r=2&oref=slogin>.

"Street and Prison Gang Member Initiations." Gangs Or Us. Web. January 2009. <http://www.gangsorus.com/initiations.html>.

The Cluetrain Manifesto. Web. April 2009. <http://www.cluetrain.com/>.

The Home Depot Home Improver Club. Web. 05 January 2009. <http://www.homeimproverclub.com/>.

The Palace of Light. Web. May 2009. <http://thepalaceoflight.com/>.

"Toyota Sequoia." Wikipedia. Web. June 2009. <http://en.wikipedia.org/wiki/Toyota_Sequoia>.

Vella, Matt. "Inside Toyota's Hybrid Truck." BusinessWeek. 28 December 2007. Web. December 2007.<http://www.businessweek.com/innovate/content/dec2007/id20071221_761295.htm>.

"What makes Google great." CNNMoney.com. 09 January 2007. Web. May 2008. <http://money.cnn.com/video/fortune/2008/01/22/bpw.google.fortune/>.

Williams, Roy H. The Wizard of Ads. Texas: Bard Press, 1998. Secret Formulas of the Wizard of Ads. Texas: Bard Press, 1999. "Time and Chance." 17 December 2007. Web. 17 December 2007. <http://www.mondaymorningmemo.com/?ShowMe=ThisMemo&MemoID=1730>.

"Yvon Chouinard." Wikipedia. Web. 19 August 2009. <http://en.wikipedia.org/wiki/Yvon_Chouinard>.

Zahavi, Amotz and Avishag Zahavi. The Handicap Principle. New York: Oxford University Press, 1997.

What is Wizard Academy?

Composed of a fascinating series of workshops led by some of the most accomplished instructors in America, Wizard Academy is a progressive new kind of business and communications school whose stated objective is to improve the creative thinking and communication skills of sales professionals, internet professionals, business owners, educators, ad writers, ministers, authors, inventors, journalists and CEOs.

Founded in 1999, the Academy has exploded into a worldwide phenomenon with an impressive fraternity of alumni who are rapidly forming an important worldwide network of business relationships.

"Alice in Wonderland on steroids! I wish Roy Williams had been my very first college professor. If he had been, everything I learned after that would have made a lot more sense and been a lot more useful... Astounding stuff."

— Dr. Larry McCleary,
Neurologist and Theoretical Physicist

"...Valuable, helpful, insightful, and thought provoking. We're recommending it to everyone we see."

— Jan Nations and Sterling Tarrant
senior managers, Focus on the Family

"Be prepared to take a wild, three-ring-circus journey into the creative recesses of the brain...[that] will change your approach to managing and marketing your business forever. For anyone who must think critically or write creatively on the job, the Wizard Academy is a must."

—Dr. Kevin Ryan
Pres., The Executive Writer

"Even with all I knew, I was not fully prepared for the experience I had at the Academy... Who else but a wizard can make sense of so many divergent ideas? I highly recommend it."

—Mark Huffman,
Advertising Production Manager, Procter & Gamble

"A life-altering 72 hours."

—Jim Rubart

*To learn more about Wizard Academy,
visit www.WizardAcademy.com or
call the academy at (800) 425-4769*